**Capital
Gaines LLC**

MY ADVICE

RELATIONS CONNOISSEUR

MARCUS E. SANDERS

Capital
Gaines LLC

CAPITAL GAINES LLC

Copyright © 2024 by Capital Gaines LLC.

All rights reserved.

No portion of this book may be reproduced in any form without written permission from the publisher or author, except as permitted by U.S. copyright law.

This publication is designed to provide accurate and authoritative information in regard to the subject matter covered. It is sold with the understanding that neither the author nor the publisher is engaged in rendering legal, investment, accounting or other professional services. While the publisher and author have used their best efforts in preparing this book, they make no representations or warranties with respect to the accuracy or completeness of the contents of this book and specifically disclaim any implied warranties of merchantability or fitness for a particular purpose. No warranty may be created or extended by sales representatives or written sales materials. The advice and strategies contained herein may not be suitable for your situation. You should consult with a professional when appropriate. Neither the publisher nor the author shall be liable for any loss of profit or any other commercial damages, including but not limited to special, incidental, consequential, personal, or other damages.

CapitalGaines LLC Wilmington DE 19807

Email: rg@capitalgaines.com Website: www.capgainesllc.com Phone: 302-433-6777

Book Cover by Marcus Sanders

Editor Andrea Gaines

ISBN- 979-8-9876581-3-0 edition 2024

Acknowledgements

First and foremost,

Thank you for allowing me to assist you on this journey.

Every time you pick this book up you will get a new tool to put in your toolbox so that you maybe able to navigate thru this journey of a sound and firm understanding of your mate.

I want to thank God, my wife and my kids for sticking with me and being here for me.

I appreciate all the love.

Marcus Sanders

Contents

Foreword	XV
Introduction	XIX
Title Page	XXIII
1. ASK YOURSELF	1
2. THINGS A WOMAN SHOULD KNOW	3
3. MEN AND WOMEN CAN BE	5
4. WOMEN AND MEN LISTEN	7
5. MEN AND WOMEN LISTEN	9
6. LOVE DOESN'T OR ISN'T	13
7. WOMEN NEED TO BE OR HAVE	15
8. WOMEN NEED TO BE OR HAVE	17
9. NEVER ASSUME	19
10. SIMPLY, MEN	21
11. SIMPLY, MEN	23
12. SIMPLY MEN	25
13. MEN LISTEN AND UNDERSTAND	27

14.	MEASURING YOUR RELATIONSHIP	29
15.	COMMUNICATION TIPS	31
16.	QUESTIONS	33
17.	CONSERNING SEX	35
18.	SOME THINGS TO REMEMBER	37
19.	THINGS A WOMAN SHOULD KNOW	39
About the author		43
Also by		53

Foreword

My Advice is not just a book; it's a guide, a mentor, and a companion for anyone seeking to navigate the complex waters of a romantic relationships. With the precision of a connoisseur, Marcus dives into the complex dynamics that make or break a relationship. His insights are practical, rooted in real-life experiences, with a deep understanding of human nature.

He begins by prompting us to ask questions about ourselves and our relationships, giving us a level of self-awareness that is important for personal growth and relational success. His approach is both direct and compassionate.

For women, he provides a roadmap to understanding the nature of men. For men, he dispels the myth that compassion and patience are a weakness for men, urging them to embrace these qualities as strengths that can enhance their relationships.

My Advice is a call to action to engage fully and sincerely in your relationships.

As you read through the pages of this book, Marcus's wisdom will inspire you to strive for a relationship that is not just surviving but thriving—a relationship that is truly fulfilling for both partners.

Whether you're just starting out in a new relationship, seeking to improve a long-term partnership, or wanting to understand love better, My Advice is a valuable resource.

Allow Marcus E. Sanders to guide you on this journey to a healthier, more fulfilling relationship.

-Gaines

INTRODUCTION

Dear.

Allow yourself a moment to forget about what you think for just a minute and allow yourself to just take a minute to read and digest these few choice words I have laid on these lines so that you may receive this gift of understanding and life's lessons.

If your looking for a cheat sheet, here is my gift to you all.

"Take my Advice or be a sacrifice in the journey of self-awareness of your own assumptions of what men think."

—— **Marcus E. Sanders**

My Advice

Relations Connoisseur

Marcus E. Sanders

Capital Gaines LLC

Capital Gaines LLC

1

ASK YOURSELF

Ask yourself: what are you looking for in a relationship or your relationship?

Ask yourself: do you honestly know what it takes to have a healthy fulfilling relationship?

Ask yourself: if you're willing to do what it takes to have a successful relationship?

Ask yourself: if you can be strong enough for the both of you when the time arises? Eventually that time will come!

Ask yourself: where your relationship is heading, if anywhere? Where do you really want it to go?

Ask yourself: if you really know your mate as a person? In most instances the answer is usually "No"

2

THINGS A WOMAN SHOULD KNOW

Most men think they know what they want. When they receive it they find something wrong with it.

So, women you have to be firm and truly stable, because most men really don't have a clue as to what a relationship consists of. He's like a kid with a new toy, once the newness wears off it's no longer appealing. Now it's your job to remind him why your toys the best.

Men always go after what they want, instead of what they need, see he's really a kid at heart and needs a strong woman to bring him to his fullest potential.

Ladies this is a task that is yours for the taking. Apply yourselves properly and you will see the diamond shine. A man is only as good as his woman.

A man is really a very complex, yet simple creature. Complex because of what society says he should be or do. This is a total conflict with what a man needs to do to be a husband or a productive partner in his relationship. You need to coach him into knowing what is needed to make your relationship work. Nine out of ten men don't have a clue as to what they want. It's hard work but the rewards are lovely.

3

MEN AND WOMEN CAN BE

Selfish, Unresponsive, Unsupportive, Unappreciative, Inconsiderate, Unforgiving

---

These are the characteristics of a single person, some come naturally, due to past experiences, relationships etc.

It's hard to break some of these habits but with a conscious mind and an open line of communication they all can be understood and modified.

When you find yourself in a relationship you will have to change your attitude about a lot of things because it's not just you anymore.

So, remember that because it will help you in a lot of situations you will find yourself in.

4

WOMEN AND MEN LISTEN

First and foremost, you both need to understand that it takes two to participate fully, in order to have a successful relationship. Only through struggle will you grow to appreciate each other as partners in your relationship.

It's a process of growth and healthy development. It's two people who think they know each other that really don't. There's always one who is reserved in giving up all of one's self. Fear of being let down or hurt. It's a matter of protecting one's self from failure. It just happens that way, but there's a reason and with time and patience you will knock down those walls. Everyone has issues, some bigger than others.

Time and patience will allow the relationship to grow to its fullest potential. Only, if you're willing to work for it. Remember being selfish is counterproductive to your growth. Always communicate, not at your mate, but with your mate. The goal is to have a happy, healthy fulfilling relationship. So, remember to keep the line of communication open.

5

MEN AND WOMEN LISTEN

Understanding
Ask yourself: if you can be understanding? In the situation you feel you can't. Ask yourself why? Is it pride, ego or selfishness that's stopping you?

These are questions you'll have to ask yourself so you may apply yourself appropriately in those situations that need sincere understanding.

Honesty
Can you be honest? Little lies turn into big lies. If you can't be truthful, you will have a problem trying to remember the lies you told. Would you want your mate lying to you? You don't hurt people you love.

Be An Attentive Listener

When you truly listen to your mate you gather information that helps you understand what he/she is going through and what you can do to help.

Attention men: always remember this one.

Trusting

Most people have a problem with trust. Their afraid of being hurt or let down and these things will happen when you're dealing with people.

If you adapt the attitude of: I am going to put sincere effort forward and if it doesn't work it not my fault.

Now if you don't give it your very best effort, you then are giving yourself that much more room for failure.

In order to have a successful relationship you have to be trusting, but don't be a fool.

Don't let past experiences block your vision.

Most people who aren't trusting have been either let down, hurt or disappointed. It could also be that they themselves are not to be trusted.

It's time to trust yourself!

6

LOVE DOESN'T OR ISN'T

Disrespectful
Abusive, physically or mentally
Degrading
Unappreciative

The person displaying any of these attributes has issues within themselves that are destructive and counterproductive to the growth of any relationship.

Advice:
Seek professional help or talk about it and express the effects that it is having on you and the relationship.

"A relationship is a beautiful fulfilling agreement between two people."

7

WOMEN NEED TO BE OR HAVE

Have patience and be patient Be understanding
Keep an open line of communication (being open leads to proper mutual understanding) Remain honest.

Be truly dedicated Understand commitment fully Be strong willed, yet balanced Respect yourself (at all times)

Be appreciative

Respect his faults (no one's perfect) Be unselfish

Be sincere

Understand and respect his frustrations (you're his support system)

Be his best friend Don't be blind (life is about making tough choices)

Never assume "Ask".

8

WOMEN NEED TO BE OR HAVE

Women you are the key to the success. You're the one who needs to be the strongest and most understanding until you cultivate him into what he professes to be.

Compassion is the key.

He's not your enemy even though in some instances it seems that way. He needs your relentless efforts in establishing the healthy, fulfilling relationship you deserve.

You only get what you strive for.

Remember men are stubborn, so be tactful in delicate situations concerning his ego and pride.

9

NEVER ASSUME

Assuming your mate should know, is very harmful to a relationship. Men are very forgetful. Women remember their very first kiss.

The very first time you said "I Love You". All her precious moments, they're her moments because she holds them sacred and feels you should too! Ladies if he doesn't remember, it doesn't mean he doesn't care. Men simply don't compute those moments like you do. Now if you ask him who won the Superbowl in 2003, you can expect him to remember and practically relive that moment.

Always ask or speak about what's important to you, if you don't know or understand something ASK, NEVER ASSUME.

Don't have the attitude, he/she should know. That attitude is counterproductive to growth.

Always, always keep in mind, your objective is to have a healthy, successful, fulfilling relationship.

Commitment and collaboration, positive change is possible.

10

SIMPLY, MEN

I am about to enlighten you on the qualities you need to have and implement in your relationship. Your full participation will allow the relationship to grow rapidly. It will not grow healthy or productive without you, so be an active partner.

Mainly be mentally capable. Women are emotional creatures and if you're not a listener, you will not be able to hear when you are in a situation that calls for silence, a nod of the head or a smile of assurance. Now if you're impatient and think she's supposed to follow you in every instance you're really crazy and in need of a psychic. Remember she is a person who has a brain and her own issues and it's your job to be aware of your mate at all times. Physically and emotionally, now listen!

Understanding your role as a partner/husband in the relationship/marriage gives you stability and productivity.

Communication is the key to a fulfilling relationship, so always keep the line of communication wide open.

If you don't know, ask? It's that simple.

NEVER ASSUME ANYTHING!

She's not your enemy, she's your best friend. She's your partner and she needs your participation all the time to make it work.

11

SIMPLY, MEN

Be understanding Be honest

Be a professional listener Learn compassion (it's a must) Be patient and have patience (men have the "now" attitude)

Be committed as a partner (she can't do it alone and neither can you) Keep the level of respect high

Be trusting (no trust, no growth only misery) Be sincere (all the time)

Be encouraging Learn to be unselfish Be supportive (she has point of views, she's also a person) Respect her faults

No one's perfect, there may be something about her you don't like, but I bet there's something about you she doesn't like either

Be willing to compromise

12

SIMPLY MEN

Compassion

Men look at compassion as a weakness. I am here to tell you it's a strength, because it will help you understand her a lot better or the way she feels about certain situations.

When you were a little boy and fell down and hurt yourself your dad told you to get up and stop crying. If your sister fell down and scraped her knee, he's all over her, that's his baby girl. We are taught to be tough, but you don't have to be tough with your mate. Pops showed selective compassion.

Patience

You have to be patient in order to allow the relationship to grow. Everything doesn't happen overnight, even though we think it should.

Commitment

Be committed fully, not just a paycheck and the occasional yard work. Be emotionally aware of your woman. Men seem to fold under pressure. Be a committed partner, she can't do it by herself and she isn't your enemy. Even though she may complain sometimes, evidently there's something wrong. It's your job to find out what it is and to fix it. That's what you do, right, you fix things!

13

MEN LISTEN AND UNDERSTAND

Understand that a woman needs you to "listen" to her when she's talking. She is telling you something she wants you to hear. She's not talking just to be talking, even though you may think so. "Always" make time for her because she's sharing valuable information with you, you just don't know it.

Understand her weaknesses and respect them, never exploit them. Help her to grow stronger.

Most men forget that their mate is a person first. A person that has her own thoughts, views and personality. So remember she's a person first and appreciate that fact. Instead of the attitude, you know what's best and that may be true, but not in all instances. Understand that she needs you to be open and trusting, so that you can truly receive the joy and dedication she will bring to the relationship. Men need to be reminded that relationships are team efforts, and that he can't do it all by himself even though he'll try.

Money makes people think they run the house, when it's really a false sense of security. Remember it's "US" not "I", no matter who the bread winner is.

14

MEASURING YOUR RELATIONSHIP

Weathering the so called uncomfortable or bad situations that occur in a relationship will measure the strength in your relationship.

There will always be ups and downs, but the way you handle them will let you know if your relationship was strengthened or weakened. Then you need to look and see what you need to work on to make it better.

Never shut down communication, but respect your partners moments of silence and noncooperation. Be patient. One of you has to be the stronger while the other is being unresponsive.

"You only get what you strive for"

15

COMMUNICATION TIPS

Most people aren't very expressive, especially pertaining to the opposite sex. How do you expect the person to understand or respect your point of view if you're scared to say what's needed to help your partner know and understand you. If your unable to be open and honest then the secrets will always block the path of true happiness. It's time to trust, I understand being afraid, but if you don't have true communication, then you only have a disastrous unfulfilling one-sided association. A relationship is a two-way partnership with input from both sides.

Try This

Ask your mate what their idea of a relationship is? You both write down what you think. You now have an idea of what the other thinks. This will open the door for communication and it will give you a good idea of your mate's point of view.

16

QUESTIONS

Men Ask Yourselves?
If you had a daughter, would you want her to be involved or married to a man like you? If not then there are some issues you need work on. What's so great is that you're willing to work on those things.

Always give your best, your mate deserves that.

Women Ask Yourselves?

If you had a son, would you want him to be involved or marry a woman like you? Again, if not there are issues you need to work on. It's especially hard for a woman to take a step back and look at herself for errors. Well, it's not errors you're looking for, you're looking for clues that hinder and stagnate your relationship. These things could be as simple as, an attitude change, a decision not to ride him so hard on a conflicting issue that's really small. With a sincere approach and consistency, you will find answers easily.

17

CONSERNING SEX

Mutual communication pertaining to sexual preferences is the ultimate key to a fulfilling sex life. Men, we have the grave misconception that we know what women want. Well, we really don't have a clue, unless she tells us. Simple fact, it's her body and she knows what works. So, ask her!

Women, your man is sexually aroused all the time and has a very active sexual appetite. Many are hesitant about verbalizing his likes and dislikes. So if he doesn't speak about anything specific take that as a sign that he is uncomfortable talking about sexual desires. So ask him!

Have you ever heard or asked "How Was That", "Did You Like That" or "Was That As Good For You As It Was For Me"?

Take that as a sign, Either he's not sure of himself or he's not in tune with your body.

The body will speak for itself.

"Communication and details are the key"

18

SOME THINGS TO REMEMBER

*A*sk yourself: what are you looking for in a relationship or your relationship?

Ask yourself: do you honestly know what it takes to have a healthy fulfilling relationship?

Ask yourself: if you're willing to do what it takes to have a successful relationship?

Ask yourself: if you can be strong enough for the both of you when the time arises? Eventually that time will come!

Ask yourself: where your relationship is heading, if anywhere? Where do you really want it to go?

Ask yourself: if you really know your mate as a person? In most instances the answer is usually "No"

19

THINGS A WOMAN SHOULD KNOW

Consistency is imperative. In order to have a successful relationship, you have to be consistent in whatever you did or didn't do that got you to this point.

See when you first start dating, you're excited, you're romantic, you're thoughtful, you're a listener, you're understanding. Once your together for a while you no longer do all those things. Then you wonder why your mate isn't as excited about things or reserved, it's because you've changed.

Always remember what made your mate special to you on that very first encounter.

Keep excitement in your relationship.

Most importantly, always keep the level of appreciation visible!

ABOUT THE AUTHOR

Marcus Sanders, is a committed husband, father, Carpenter, and Project Director for Returning Citizens Association.

A skilled carpenter by trade, Marcus is not only adept at his craft but also a proud member of the union in California. Marcus's expertise extends beyond the workshop; it reaches into the lives of those navigating the challenges of this world.

Marcus enjoys family time having 6 children and 14 grandchildren. He continues to contribute to the broader community, advocating for positive change and inspiring others with his story of redemption and growth. Marcus exemplifies the power of dedication, resilience, and the profound impact one individual can have on the lives of many. His commitment to fostering healthy relationships and his relentless pursuit of personal and communal betterment serve as a testament to his enduring legacy.

ONE ON ONE

If you have a question or need advice, mail or email your requests to:

Marcus Sanders

PO Box 562

1735 Robinson St

Oroville, CA 95927

Email: amaya91068@gmail.com

$10.00 - Cash App $acirescorner

Please allow time for a reply.

Capital
Gaines LLC

ALSO BY

CAPITAL GAINES LLC.

Also Available @www.amazon.com
It's Hard Being the Same. By Eric Curtis
Roxxy' By A.C. Bellard
Ideas More Powerful Than Force. By Ricky Gaines II
Triumph. By Mesro
NEOLOGIC THOUGHT: By AH'KHEMU
JR'S Alphabet Numbers Trace Book: by Richard Gaines
How To Self Publish
DeyUgo
Poetic Reflections Of Redemption
52 Weekly Christian Principles
Tapped-In Magazine

For ordering info please visit our website
www.capgainesllc.com

MARCUS E. SANDERS

Capital
Gaines LLC

Made in the USA
Columbia, SC
19 November 2024